ISBN 978-0-428-15101-0
PIBN 11249910

1 MONTH OF
FREE
READING

at

www.ForgottenBooks.com

By purchasing this book you are
eligible for one month membership to
ForgottenBooks.com, giving you
unlimited access to our entire
collection of over 1,000,000 titles via
our web site and mobile apps.

To claim your free month visit:

www.forgottenbooks.com/free1249910

English
Français
Deutsche
Italiano
Español
Português

www.forgottenbooks.com

Mythology Photography **Fiction**
Fishing Christianity **Art** Cooking
Essays Buddhism Freemasonry
Medicine **Biology** Music **Ancient**
Egypt Evolution Carpentry Physics
Dance Geology **Mathematics** Fitness
Shakespeare **Folklore** Yoga Marketing
Confidence Immortality Biographies
Poetry **Psychology** Witchcraft
Electronics Chemistry History **Law**
Accounting **Philosophy** Anthropology
Alchemy Drama Quantum Mechanics
Atheism Sexual Health **Ancient History**
Entrepreneurship Languages Sport
Paleontology Needlework Islam
Metaphysics Investment Archaeology
Parenting Statistics Criminology
Motivational

aHD9001
.A37
c.2

United States
Department of
Agriculture

Foreign
Agricultural
Service

Circular Series

ATH 8-90
August 1990

AGRICULTURAL TRADE HIGHLIGHTS

June Exports Surprisingly Strong For 'Slow' Month; Imports Decline

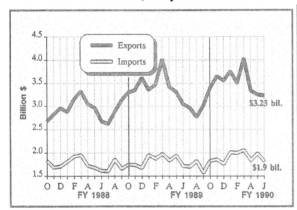

U.S. agricultural exports in June were surprisinly strong for what is normally a slow month. Imports declined slightly although they remained on course for a record high.

June trade data released by the Commerce Department on August 17 placed U.S. agricultural exports at $3.23 billion and 11.7 million metric tons, relatively unchanged from May's level of $3.25 billion. However, compared with June of 1989, this month's export total was up nearly $200 million.

June's performance brought the cumulative export total (October-June) for fiscal 1990 to $31.7 billion and 119.2 million tons. This is an increase of about 3 percent in value and 4 percent in volume.

Significant commodity gains in June from year-ago levels came from cotton (up 148 percent to $192 million), soybean meal (up 97 percent to $84 million), tree nuts (up 105 percent to $67 million), and soybean oil (up 135 percent to $45 million). Declines for the month were not large enough to offset the gains but they did come in major categories such as corn (down 7 percent to $636 million), wheat (down 16 percent to $341 million), feeds and fodders (down 15 percent to $129 million), and rice (down 20 percent to $52 million).

Japan continued to be the largest market in June, at $596 million, although it did drop 9 percent from June 1989. Canada was second with $388 million, edging out the Soviet Union at $385 million. Other top five markets were the European Community (EC) with $378 million and South Korea with $231 million.

The largest gains continue to come from sales to Canada (mainly due to the new data reporting system), up $150 million, followed by the Soviet Union, up $44 million, and the EC, up $36 million.

Agricultural imports for June totaled $1.9 billion, down $114 million from May but up $156 million from June 1989. For fiscal 1990-to-date, imports totaled $17.3 billion, up nearly $1 billion from last year. Imports are projected to reach a record level of $22.5 billion by year end.

This month's issue includes two special reports. The Country Spotlight on page 5--a regular report initiated this month--is on Mexico, always an important market. On page 13 is the trade record of how much the EC and U.S. spend each year on agriculture.

U.S. Agricultural Export Summaries
October-June and Latest Month Comparisons

Product Summary

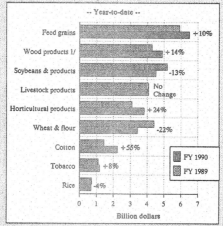

-- Year-to-date --

Product	Change
Feed grains	+10%
Wood products 1/	+14%
Soybeans & products	-13%
Livestock products	No Change
Horticultural products	+24%
Wheat & flour	-22%
Cotton	+55%
Tobacco	+8%
Rice	-4%

FY 1990
FY 1989

Billion dollars

Feed grains
Wood products 1/
Soybeans & products
Livestock products
Horticultural products
Wheat & flour
Cotton
Tobacco
Rice

0

Top Ten Markets Summary

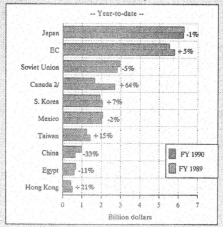

-- Year-to-date --

Japan	-1%
EC	+5%
Soviet Union	-5%
Canada 2/	+64%
S. Korea	+7%
Mexico	-2%
Taiwan	+15%
China	-33%
Egypt	-11%
Hong Kong	+21%

FY 1990
FY 1989

Billion dollars

Market	
Japan	
EC	
Soviet Union	
Canada 2/	
S. Korea	
Mexico	
Taiwan	
China	-1
Egypt	-44
Hong Kong	+4

0   100

Note: Percentages are computed as the change from a year ago.

1/ Not included in agricultural totals. 2/ U.S. agricultural exports to Canada ha about $1 billion a year and officially recognized by both Governments. Effectiv Census began adjusting U.S. export statistics to account for these differences.

S

showed a 7-percent gain from a million metric tons registered a :arters of fiscal 1990, value rose last year's $30.8 billion while million tons from the 114-mil-

Increased sales of soybean meal and soybean oil in June led to the reversal of a trend observed throughout the year. For the first time in many months, the value of *soybean and product* exports, at $357 million, was higher than last year's monthly total. In spite of June's favorable showing, year-to-date export value of $4.5 billion is still well below last year's $5.2 billion. Taiwan remains one of the only major markets to register positive sales growth to this point in fiscal 1990.

Among major commodities, *cotton* exports experienced the largest percentage gain from a year ago. Export value of $192 million was up 148 percent due to firm U.S. prices and a 98-percent jump in volume. For the first 3 quarters of this fiscal year, the value and volume of cotton exports, totaling $2.2 billion and 1.4 million tons, is up 55 and 31 percent, respectively from October-June 1989. Advances were reported in sales to all principal markets.

Unmanufactured tobacco sales soared for the month, rising 30 percent in value from last June to $89 million and 7 percent in volume to 13,000 tons. Cumulative-to-date exports to four of the top five markets have climbed, reaching $1.2 billion and 189,000 tons.

A drop in exports of animal fat and hides and skins was partly responsible for the 5-percent decline in the value of *livestock* sales from June of a

year ago. For the month, the value livestock exports measured $427 r lion, bringing fiscal year-to-date sa to $4.1 billion. Much of the 92-p cent gain in cumulative exports Canada this year appears to be result of changes in the data repc ing system. On the other hand, ports to Mexico are down 28 perc largely because of lower shipments live cattle, hides, and variety meat.

Continuing strong prices for t nuts, nursery products, cut flowe and some fruits and vegetables c tributed to the 43-percent upsurge exports of *horticultural produ* Sales in June amounted to $521 r lion and 569,000 tons compared $364 million and 530,000 tons a y ago. The value of fiscal year expc now totals $3.8 billion while volu sums to 4.6 million tons. Both sho finish the year at record levels. far, the largest increase for the y has been in sales to Canada, mainly to statistical reporting c ges.

For yet another month, exports *wood products* scored an impres gain with sales rising 9 percen value. These increases brought cumulative value of wood export $4.9 billion. All major markets tinue to show advances in fiscal sales. Like horticultural products, ports of wood products should fi the year at a record level.

For more information, con Katheen Anderson, (202) 382-9055

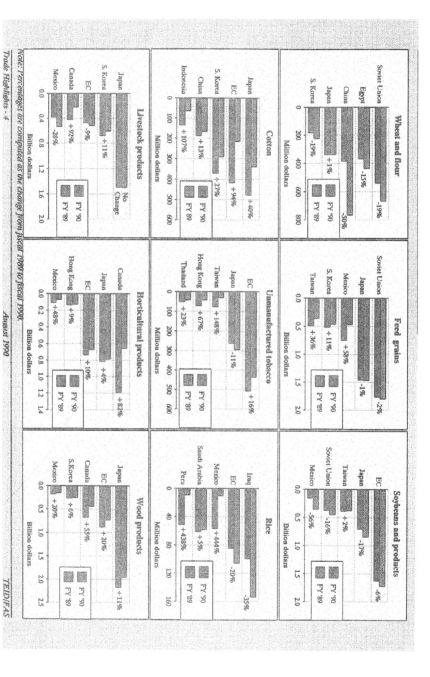

Note: Percentages are computed as the change from fiscal 1989 to fiscal 1990.

August 1990

Country Spotlight: Mexico

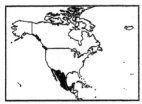

With a market size of 86 million consumers who are becoming wealthier as a result of the country's economic recovery, Mexico appears to be a land of opportunity for U.S. exporters of agricultural products.

In calendar 1989, Mexico was a particularly good market for the United States. Sales of $2.7 billion made Mexico the fourth largest importer of U.S. agricultural products. U.S. exports that year were nearly $500 million higher than in 1988 due to the reluctance of Mexican producers to market goods under their government's price constraints. Significant U.S. sales to Mexico in 1989 included corn ($435 million), grain sorghum ($274 million), soybeans ($271 million), dairy products ($195 million), seeds ($131 million), and animal fats ($102 million). Favorable export opportunities exist for processed products, red meat, poultry, and rice.

U.S. agricultural trade with Mexico has increased substantially in the past few years due to the country's improving economic situation, strengthening currency, significant use of GSM credit guarantees ($1.5 billion in GSM-102 in fiscal 1990), and accession to the GATT in 1986. In addition, Mexico's domestic production problems and its recent trade liberalization efforts have raised U.S. exports to the country. As a result, the United States' presence in the Mexican import market has risen from a 69-percent market share in 1986 to a 75-percent share in 1989.

Mexico is still in the process of recovering from a severe drought which raised the country's imports of U.S. wheat, sorghum, barley, and beans in 1989. The continuing effects of the drought will keep U.S. exports of corn and sorghum high. For the third quarter of this fiscal year, exports of corn and sorghum are already up 70 and 40 percent, respectively, over the same period in fiscal 1989. Also, decreased irrigation water supplies in one of Mexico's major wheat and soybean production regions will heighten prospects for increased U.S. sales of these products throughout the year.

Mexican imports will continue to be affected by the country's domestic policy changes. In 1989, the Mexican government liberalized livestock and sorghum trade and production, a move which should result in higher Mexican imports of these items. In fact, the liberalization of livestock trade has, in part, caused Mexico's purchases of lamb to rise 48 percent. In addition, the recent termination of both the country's monopoly on sugar marketing and its production support policy led sugar imports from the United States to reach $60 million in the first half of this calendar year, more than double the total for the same period last year.

Expected future policy changes which reduce trade barriers will likely have a similar positive effect on Mexican imports, making the country an even more attractive market for U.S. products. Other factors which should contribute to strong Mexican imports from the United States include continued economic growth, greater consumer purchasing power, limited opportunities for expansion of domestic grain and oilseed production, increased tourism, opening of high-value food and beverage markets, continued availability of GSM credit guarantees, and competitive U.S. commodity prices.

For more information, contact
Kathleen Anderson, (202) 382-9055.

Status of U.S.-Mexico Free Trade Agreement (FTA)

On August 8, U.S. Trade Representative Carla Hills and Mexican Secretary of Commerce and Industrial Development Dr. Jaime Serra Puche jointly recommended to Presidents Bush and Salinas the formal initiation of negotiations on a comprehensive FTA. They agreed that an FTA should lead to the progressive elimination of impediments to trade in goods, services, and investment, as well as to the protection of intellectual property rights and the establishment of fair and expeditious dispute settlement procedures. President Bush is expected to notify Congress formally when it reconvenes in September of the intent of the United States and Mexico to negotiate on an FTA.

Recognizing that certain sectors within the agricultural community have concerns about the potential implications of a U.S.-Mexico FTA, negotiations in this regard will be managed very carefully to ensure that the agreement not only maximizes 2-way trade benefits, but does so in a mutually beneficial manner for both the United States and Mexico. USDA will conduct a comprehensive analysis of the implications of a U.S.-Mexico FTA for the agricultural sector.

U.S. agricultural imports for June totaled $1.9 billion, down 6 percent from May, but up 9 percent from a year ago. This was the highest level on record for the month of June and brings the fiscal year-to-date total to $17.3 billion, up $1 billion from the same period a year ago.

Competitive product imports have been strong all year and for June measured $1.4 billion, up 12 percent from a year ago. Cumulative imports through June were up $1.1 billion, or 10 percent, from last year.

Large increases of some imports were seen in June. Fruits were up 40 percent from a year ago, raising the total 10 percent above last fiscal year. Sharp increases in grape imports accounted for about 80 percent of the rise, as shipments from Chile rebounded from last year's depressed levels. Likewise, vegetable imports

June imports at highest level on record.

were up 51 percent from May. So far this year vegetable imports are up $480 million, with tomatoes accounting for half of the increase.

Live cattle imports during the year were up 34 percent, or $210 million, from last year. Imports from Mexico and Canada account for 97 percent of U.S. imports of live cattle. Live cattle account for 95 percent of live animal imports.

Some imports showed large declines. At $110 million, wine and beer were down 34 percent from last May. Dairy and poultry imports were down 42 percent. However, stronger imports earlier this year have left the total for the first 9 months 5-percent above last year's level.

Noncompetitive product imports for June totaled $490 million, up 3 percent from last June. At $4.4 billion for the first 9 months, they are down 5 percent from last year. Coffee imports in June totaled $203 million, accounting for 40 percent of total noncompetitive imports. For the year coffee imports were up 40 percent in volume, but were down 5 percent in value from last year.

Rubber and allied gum imports for June totaled $62 million, down 10 percent from last June, bringing imports for the year to $600 million, down 30 percent, or $240 million from last year. Of this decline 70 percent is due to reduced purchases from Indonesia.

Using fiscal year-to-date import data, Guatemala has replaced the Philippines as a top 10 supplier of U.S. agricultural imports. Cumulative purchases from Guatemala have increased 68 percent, or $157 million, over last year. Increases of $90 million for coffee products and $35 million for fruits and vegetables accounted for most of the gain.

Imports from Mexico were up 35 percent, or $568 million, from last year. Sharp increases in fruit and vegetable ($339 million), live animals ($146 million), and coffee ($91 million) were largely responsible. The United States is forecast to purchase $2.5 billion worth of agricultural imports from Mexico in this fiscal year, up $500 million from last year.

For more information, contact James Johnson, (202) 382-9522.

Noncompetitive imports do not compete with U.S. production and include: bananas/plantains, coffee (incl. processed), cocoa (incl. processed), rubber/allied gums, spices, essential oils, tea, and carpet wools. All other imports are classified as competitive.

U.S. Agricultural Imports by Major Product Sector
June 1990 Versus Month-ago and Year-ago

Import Category	June 1990	Month Ago	Year Ago	% Change From May'90	% Change From June'89
	— Million $ —				
Total competitive	1,372	1,463	1,228	-6	12
Fruits, incl. juices	201	212	143	-5	40
Wines & beer	110	167	161	-34	-32
Vegetables	238	158	148	51	60
Beef & veal	120	145	135	-17	-11
Dairy/poultry	52	89	70	-42	-25
Pork	60	74	68	-19	-11
Total noncompetitive	490	512	477	-4	3
Coffee & products	203	162	187	25	9
Cocoa & products	81	123	65	-34	22
Bananas/plantains	72	91	73	-21	-1
Rubber/allied gums	62	55	69	13	-10
Spices	20	23	30	-13	-33
Tea	10	14	11	-29	-9
Total agri. imports	1,862	1,976	1,706	-6	9

Source: Commodity Trade Analysis Branch, Economic Research Service, U.S. Department of Agriculture, Washington, D.C.

U.S. Agricultural Import Summaries
October-June and Latest Month Comparisons

Product Summary

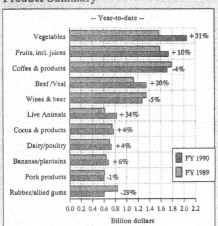

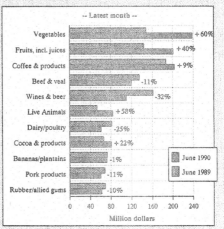

Top Ten Suppliers Summary

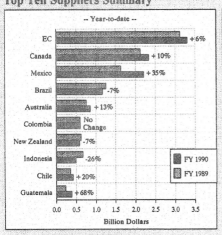

Note: Percentages are computed as the change from a year ago.

Trade Policy Updates

GATT Negotiations Enter Final Phase

Uruguay Round Negotiations on Agriculture, under the General Agreement on Tariffs and Trade (GATT), have entered their final, most intensive phase. Participating countries have until the first week of December 1990 to finalize an agreement detailing how world agricultural policy is to be reformed. In meeting this challenge, countries have agreed to work on the basis of a document prepared by Aart de Zeeuw, Chairman of the Agriculture Negotiating Group (ANG). De Zeeuw's text calls for countries to agree to reductions in agricultural support and protection in four separate policy areas: market access, internal support, export subsidies, and sanitary and phytosanitary measures. Because the document provides an attempt to find common ground, nearly every country can find some part of the text with which it is uncomfortable. Nevertheless, the United States believes that the text provides a good basis for the final phase of the negotiations.

The ANG will continue to meet through the beginning of December 1990, attempting to complete the details of a final agreement and to explore areas left unsettled by the chairman's text. As part of this work, countries have agreed to submit comprehensive "country lists" identifying specific policies subject to negotiations. These lists will include such basic data as the tariff equivalents of existing non-tariff barriers, the level of internal support for individual commodities, and the current level of export subsidization. The Uruguay Round will end with a final meeting at the ministerial level in Brussels, beginning December 3.

EC Refuses To Impose Countervailing Duties On Corn Gluten Feed

The European Community Commission has turned down a 1988 petition, initiated by France, to impose countervailing duties (CVD's) on EC imports of U.S. corn gluten feed. Strong U.S. opposition and limited support in the EC were effective in blocking the French attempt to impose CVD's.

U.K. Committee Recommends Against BST Application

The United Kingdom's Veterinary Products Committee (VPC) has provisionally agreed to recommend that Monsanto's application for a commercial license for Bovine Somatotropin (BST) be turned down based on concerns of quality and animal safety, including animal welfare in relation to the commercial application of the product. The VPC's initial decision against BST is subject to review and confirmation by the committee at its next meeting on September 13, 1990. In a subsequent press release, Monsanto expressed confidence that further submissions of data on dairy cow safety through the VPC appeals procedure will resolve all remaining concerns on BST.

Payment Plan Specified For Portugal EC Grain Regime Agreement

Additional income for Portuguese producers, resulting from the Portugal EC Grain Regime Agreement, will be paid on a per ton of production basis co-financed by the EC and Portugal. Under the agréement previously agreed to, the EC will prolong by 5 years the accession transition arrangements for Portugal's cereal sector. This means that Portuguese producers will continue to receive higher-than-EC prices until 2001. Wheat imports will continue to be subject to accession compensatory amounts to help ease the financial burden. Domestic market prices, on the other hand, will fall to EC levels in January 1991, thus addressing the major concern of the livestock industry.

Ontario and Ukraine Sign Agro-Industry Understanding

On July 24, the Canadian province of Ontario and the USSR's Ukraine signed a memorandum of understanding on agro-industrial activities. Both sides agreed to cooperate in the development of joint ventures in the areas of agriculture and food production, storage, processing, and marketing. Plans are already underway for a joint venture in the area of cattle breeding and artificial insemination. Other firms from Ontario are looking at potential joint ventures in crop storage and waste reduction.

East and West Germany Lift Trade Restrictions

On July 19, the Agriculture Ministry for the Federal Republic of Germany (FRG) announced the elimination of all existing quotas and other trade limitations on raw agricultural products and processed foods traded between the two Germanies. The decision took effect on August 1. A Ministry spokesman at the time of the announcement admitted that quotas and restrictions, or "the Green Border," designed to protect both the German Democratic Republic (GDR) and FRG during this transition period were not only not working but were counterproductive.

Also, effective August 1, GDR-origin agricultural products were allowed free access to all EC member states. These products are still subject to EC quality and health requirements. In the meat sector, no GDR slaughter plants meet EC standards, although FRG processed foods using GDR-origin raw product will likely be shipped to other EC member states. Surplus GDR hogs, which are estimated to number up to 1 million head, may also be exported via the FRG with EC export subsidies, primarily to the USSR and, to a lesser extent, Eastern Europe. Grain intervention buying started during August in the GDR, a month earlier than in the FRG.

EC Refuses Extension for Prior Processed Pork From Delisted Plant

The EC's Standing Veterinary Committee has refused to permit entry of 200,000 pounds (90,719 kilograms) of pork products manufactured by Farmstead Foods Corporation prior to the July 31, 1990, delistment of the plant. U.S. officials and plant representatives argued that the deadline should be based on production date and not on the "arrive by" date. In its import program, USDA's Food Safety and Inspection Service permits entry of products from delisted plants and countries as long as the product was certified before the disqualification date.

EC Increases Export Restitutions for Dairy Products

In the face of rising dairy intervention stocks (160,000 tons of skim milk powder and 140,000 tons of butter), the EC has instituted higher export refunds for dairy products, including a 40-percent increase in the refund for nonfat dry milk. The increase in the export refunds took effect July 20. EC traders voiced alarm when New Zealand underbid EC exporters by $150 per ton for a Venezuelan tender for 20,000 tons of whole milk powder. The EC considers Venezuela a traditional market for its dairy products.

The EC's increase in restitutions has reduced the price of its butter almost to the GATT minimum price and leaves little margin to increase refunds without contravening the GATT agreement. The EC is expected to seek a reduction in the International Dairy Agreement's minimum prices when members of agreement meet in September.

Mexico Removes Import Permit Requirements on Some Products

The July 17, 1990, Mexican Federal Register announced the elimination of import permit requirements for various oilseeds, oilseed flours, and animal and vegetable fat products. The order became effective on July 18. Import license requirements were eliminated for 22 tariff line items. U.S. exports of these products totaled approximately $70 million in calendar 1989.

FAS Publications

- Trading With Eastern Europe (Articles from AgExporter magazine)
- Trade Policies and Market Opportunities for U.S. Farm Products Countering Unfair Foreign Competition Through Trade and Agricultural Legislation

Requests for copies of FAS publications and Fact Sheets may be sent to the Trade Assistance and Planning Office, Foreign Agricultural Service, 3101 Park Center Drive, Suite 1103, Alexandria, VA 22302. Tel: (703) 756-6001. FAX: (703) 756-6124.

Market Updates

EC Aggressively Exporting Wheat

The European Community has begun an unusually aggressive soft wheat sales program by issuing export licenses on a record 1.9 million tons in just the first 3 weeks of the new marketing year. Licenses issued by this time last year, before the EC went on to post record wheat exports, only covered 340,000 tons; prior years averaged 160,000 tons. Brussels is apparently under strong pressure from exporters and producer co-ops to be more aggressive. At a regular weekly meeting on July 26, Brussels approved restitutions that were $3 to $5 higher than those rejected last week. This came only a few days after high-level assurances that the EC would "hold the line" for at least the next week or two.

Fast Food Companies Switch to New Oil Blend

McDonald's, Burger King, and Wendy's have announced that they will start cooking their french-fried and hash-browned potatoes in pure vegetable oil, abandoning a blend of vegetable oil and beef tallow that has long made them a target for criticism by health activist groups. Burger King was the first to announce the change, saying on July 17 it would switch its shortening blend to soybean and cottonseed oil. McDonald's is expected to use a cottonseed and corn oil mix and Wendy's will reportedly use an all-corn oil shortening. McDonald's has said that the change would result in potatoes with zero cholesterol and 45 percent less fat per serving than those the company previously served. Hardee's said it has had a positive consumer response to an all-soybean oil blend it began using several years ago. Preliminary estimates for the increased domestic demand for vegetable oils created by these changes range from 150 million to as much as 500 million pounds by 1991.

Caribbean Countries Not Able To Meet U.S. Sugar Quota

According to the Sugar Association of the Caribbean, sugar production in Guyana, Barbados, and St. Christopher-Nevis will be insufficient to meet their allocations under the 1989-1990 U.S. Sugar Quota. They will record a total shortfall of 44,000 tons on their quota allocations. Guyana accounts for almost 60 percent of this shortfall. The 1989-1990 quota period ends on September 30.

EC Approves Extension Of U.S.-EC Wine Accord

The EC Council has approved a 1-year extension of the 1983 U.S.-EC Wine Accord. The extension of the accord, which was to have expired on July 31, 1990, will allow U.S. exporters to continue to use simplified certification procedures and certain wine treating materials. During the extension period, the United States will seek permanent status for the certification procedure for wines shipped to the EC and permission to treat wine with those chemicals which are considered safe for human consumption.

GSM-102 Program To Mexico Increased

On July 23, Mexico's allocation under the fiscal 1990 GSM-102 Credit Guarantee Program was increased by $150 million. This included increments of $85 million to the feed grains line; $31.5 million to the oilseeds line; $10 million to the tallow, greases, and lard line; $10 million to the protein meals line; and $13.5 million to the undesignated line. Fiscal 1990 GSM-102 guarantees available for sales to Mexico now total $1,525 million.

West Germany Confirms Reports of Illegal Hormone Use in Calves

German veterinary officials reported an illegal use of DES, a hormone growth promoter banned in the United States, in a herd of 423 calves. The problem was detected in a routine ou-farm random sampling program. Of almost 100 percent of the samples tested, a "very high" number were found to be positive. The entire herd will be declared unfit for food production and destroyed. German officials continue to claim that their inspection system effectively guarantees safe meat for consumers.

t Prices
Decline

World wheat prices continue to fall due to sluggish demand and reports of higher supplies. The EC has increased restitutions by nearly $8.00/ton, bringing export prices below $100. Larger crops are expected in Canada, the EC, the Soviet Union, and the United States. Additional foreign exportable supplies and reduced import demand could mean a further build-up in U.S. wheat stocks.

ortage
oting
t Union

A shortage of cigarettes in the Soviet Union has led to riots in some cities, according to recent press reports. The shortage is the result of antiquated manufacturing equipment, a lack of foreign currency to purchase foreign cigarettes, and ethnic unrest in cigarette producing areas. A shortage of cardboard has compounded these problems, forcing all but six of the Soviet's 24 cigarette factories to shut down. A pack of foreign cigarettes is reported to sell for the equivalent of $17 to $25 on the black market. Cab drivers in large cities are asking for foreign currencies or Marlboros for payment. Because of government constraints, the USSR does not import cigarettes or unprocessed tobacco from the United States. Bulgaria is the Soviet's major supplier of imported tobacco and tobacco products.

Boycott
n Turkey

Recently, Izmir Shopkeepers and Monopoly Products Distributors Association of Turkey announced a consumer boycott on foreign-produced cigarettes and alcohol. The boycott has been called to protest a 20-percent increase in the retail cost of foreign cigarettes and to pressure foreign tobacco companies to keep their pledges to invest in Turkey. In addition, the boycott is expected to focus on the fact that the government monopoly only allows a 4-percent mark-up on foreign cigarettes, while permitting a 6-to 12-percent mark-up on domestic cigarettes. The boycott is voluntary and there are no legal mechanisms in place to enforce it. Imported cigarettes only represent 15 percent of the cigarettes consumed in Turkey, with the majority of the foreign cigarettes imported from the United States. In 1989, the United States sold $24.1 million worth of cigarettes to Turkey.

l Exports
o Rise

The timber industry is continuing to export at a rapid pace. Exports for January to May reached $2.7 billion, a 14-percent increase over the same period in 1989. Softwood logs and softwood lumber are still the two top exported products. During the first 5 months of 1990, the United States exported $868 million in logs and $574 million in lumber.

cial Cites
creased
tection

The head of the French Oilseeds Intervention Board, Jean-Claude Sabin, commented on the need for increased import protection for protein products. Noting that the EC currently satisfies only 35 percent of its vegetable protein needs, Sabin stated that the Community must fight within GATT to create an atmosphere supporting the expansion of production to a self-sufficiency level of 50 percent. This could be accomplished, he suggested, through a combination of new import protection measures (i.e. rebalancing) and enhanced production incentives (e.g. enlarged maximum guaranteed quantities under the so-called stabilizer scheme). Sabin also argued that the EC should seek to expand its presence in North Africa's vegetable oil markets, a presence which has been eroded to a reported 10-15 percent share by "subsidized" U.S. sales under the Export Enhancement Program. While a 50-percent market share in this region was feasible, Sabin indicated that the EC might accept an increase to just 30 percent, provided the United States "accepted the imposition of some duties on its non-cereal feeds and oilseeds."

Argentina Lowers Export Taxes on Agricultural Products	The Government of Argentina announced its intention last week to reduce export taxes on a broad range of agricultural products, including many oilseeds and oilseed products. The new tax level for soybeans and sunflower seed is 13 percent, down from 26 and 27 percent, respectively. This narrows the price differential between the raw crops and their finished products from 8 to 6 percent. The tax changes are unofficial until they have been reported in the government's Official Bulletin and are to be effective for the upcoming harvest. While the lower taxes, in principal, would tend to encourage area planted and reduce the incentive to export oilseeds in product form, the actual impact may be much less due to the economic uncertainty facing the country.
India Wants In On Cotton Exports	The Government of India recently decided to take steps to ensure that the country is perceived as a "stable and reliable" supplier of cotton. India's Central Committee on Export Strategy decided in June to set aside a minimum of 500,000 Indian bales (170 kilograms) per year for export. Reportedly, the cotton would be channeled to exports even if there were a shortage in the country. The Government made a similar decision in 1986 which included a stipulation to import cotton if production shortfalls threatened export commitments. The export policy was abandoned in subsequent years due to crop shortfalls.
China's Textile Exports Decreasing	Textile exports from China fell sharply during the January-July 1990 period, according to a recent China Daily newspaper article. Two successive poor crops, coupled with lower cotton imports, have affected the supply of cotton available for use by the textile sector. Cotton yarn exports are estimated at 68,627 tons, down nearly 21 percent from the same period a year earlier. Although no exact figure was cited, the same source states that exports of cotton cloth during the same time period are also estimated to be down. USDA currently forecasts the 1990/91 Chinese cotton crop at 21.0 million bales. If a crop of that size is realized, more cotton should be available for the country's textile industry.
Mexico Intends To Issue Additional Import Licenses for Apples	Mexican government officials have announced they will issue permits for an additional 3,500 tons of apple imports. Of the total, 2,000 tons are to be issued on August 9-- 1,000 tons to the wholesale trade and 1,250 tons to the retail trade. The remaining 1,250 tons are to be issued to the retail trade as soon as as the retail trade association applies for import permits. Permits will be valid for 1 month.
Amendments to Fiscal 1990 P.L. 480, Title I Programs	On July 23, Guyana's fiscal 1990 P.L. 480, Title I agreement with the United States was amended to add an additional $3 million (approximately 20,000 tons) worth of wheat sales. On the same day, Jamaica signed its second amendment to its fiscal 1990 P.L. 480, Title I agreement. The amendment added $3 million worth of wheat/wheat flour to the program. These agreements were followed on July 31 by a Philippine Title I agreement for an additional $21 million worth of soybean meal, and on July 31, by an amendment to Cote d' Ivoire's agreement for $5 million worth of milled rice. Cote d' Ivoire's Title I amendment is intended to encourage the Cote d' Ivoire to issue import licenses for U.S. brown rice. On August 2, El Salvador signed a first amendment to its fiscal 1990 P.L. 480, Title I agreement with the United States. The amendment allowed an additional $3.2 million worth of wheat/wheat flour and $2 million worth of tallow.

For more information, contact John Wade at (202) 382-9067.

Expected To Spend $36 Billion on Agriculture,
. Expenditures Dropping to $8.5 Billion

89 the European Community) spent $30.03 billion on ltural support and export ms, almost three times the billion the United States

utlays for export subsidies, d to move artificially high-commodities onto the world t, totaled $9.02 billion in 1989, ercent of the total EC agricul-udget. The EC expenditures port subsidies approached the hat the United States spent on upport and export programs.

pending on agricultural export ies to counter unfair trade tition (primarily from the EC) ted to $340 million in 1989, or cent of the total U.S. agricul-budget.

from direct budgetary outlays, onsumers paid an estimated)illion to support farmers in through high prices. Consumer

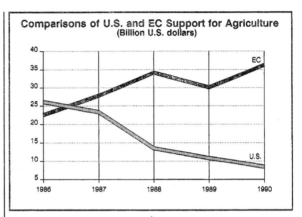

Comparisons of U.S. and EC Support for Agriculture
(Billion U.S. dollars)

transfer in the United States, on the other hand, totaled less than $15 billion.

The following table compares EC-U.S. agricultural expenditures for the past 5 years. The disparity in agricultural expenditures highlights

the lack of market orientation in EC agricultural support programs contrasted with the increasing market orientation of U.S. programs during the 1980's.

For more information, contact Emiko Miyasaka, (202) 382-9054.

Comparison of EC and U.S. Agricultural Expenditures
(Billion U.S. Dollars)

	1986	1987	1988	1989	1990e
European Community:					
Domestic Support	15.47	17.54	22.84	18.75	24.72
Export Subsidies	7.12	10.26	11.28	9.02	11.53
Total EC	22.59	27.80	34.13	30.08	36.25
United States:					
CCC Outlays	25.84	22.41	12.46	10.52	8.20
Export Subsidies	0.26	0.93	1.01	0.34	0.28
Total U.S.	26.10	23.34	13.47	10.86	8.48

1/ All EC figures converted from European Currency Units (ECUs) using the following exchange rates: Dollars/ECU=0.9837 (1986), 1.1544 (1987), 1.1825 (1988), 1.1017 (1989), 1.2059 (1990). The EC wrote off the following amounts for stock depreciation to account for expected losses at time of export: 1988, $1.47 billion; 1989, $1.59 billion; 1990, $1.77 billion (appropriated). EC figures for 1990 estimated by ERS. U.S. figures for 1990 estimated by FAS/ITP/TEID.

	October-June		
	1988/89	1989/90	Char
	-- Billion dollars --		
Grains & feeds 2/	13.028	12.730	
Wheat	4.222	3.253	
Wheat flour	0.178	0.170	
Rice	0.713	0.682	
Feed grains 3/	5.923	6.498	
Corn	5.085	5.684	
Feeds & fodders	1.406	1.396	
Oilseeds & products	6.053	5.374	
Soybeans	3.714	3.442	
Soybean meal	1.209	0.822	
Soybean oil	0.265	0.243	
Other vegetable oils	0.299	0.308	
Livestock products	4.079	4.080	
Red meats	1.617	1.609	
Animal fats	0.393	0.360	
Poultry products	0.548	0.645	
Poultry meat	0.385	0.473	
Dairy products	0.368	0.236	
Horticultural products	3.089	3.822	
Unmanufactured tobacco	1.096	1.181	
Cotton & linters	1.433	2.222	
Planting seeds	0.380	0.450	
Sugar & tropical products	0.905	1.056	
Wood products 4/	4.279	4.896	
Total agricultural export value	30.849	31.699	

	-- Mil. metric tons --		C
Grains & feeds 2/	88.085	90.053	
Wheat	26.433	20.646	
Wheat flour	0.848	0.725	
Rice	2.327	2.041	
Feed grains 3/	48.699	56.774	
Corn	41.521	49.531	
Feeds & fodders	8.552	8.397	
Oilseeds & products	18.698	20.704	
Soybeans	12.684	15.142	
Soybean meal	4.306	3.786	
Soybean oil	0.477	0.460	
Other vegetable oils	0.484	0.501	
Livestock products 5/	1.806	1.800	
Red meats	0.520	0.506	
Animal fats	1.015	0.973	
Poultry products 5/	0.350	0.444	
Poultry meat	0.346	0.441	
Dairy products 5/	0.267	0.146	
Horticultural products 5/	2.976	3.438	
Unmanufactured tobacco	0.181	0.190	
Cotton & linters	1.069	1.394	
Planting seeds	0.292	0.361	
Sugar & tropical products 5/	0.585	0.715	
Total agricultural export volume 5/	114.308	119.244	

NA = Not available.

1/ Export forecasts are from August, 1990, "Outlook for U.S. Agricultural Exp
2/ Includes pulses and corn gluten feed and meal.
3/ Includes corn, oats, barley, rye, and sorghum.
4/ Wood products are not included in agricultural product value totals.
5/ Includes only those items measured in metric tons.

Source: U.S. Bureau of the Census and August, 1990, "Outlook for U.S. Agric

Weekly Quotations for
Selected International Prices 1/

Dollars per metric ton	Week of 8/22/90	Month ago	Year ago
Wheat (c.i.f. Rotterdam) 2/			
Canadian No. 1 CWRS 13.5%	140	166	201
U.S. No. 2 DNS 14 %	138	145	184
U.S. No. 2 SRW	135	133	179
U.S. No. 3 HAD	145	154	183
Canadian No. 1 durum	158	167	193
Feed Grains (c.i.f. Rotterdam) 2/			
U.S. No. 3 yellow corn	125	133	123
Soybeans and Meal (c.i.f. Rotterdam) 2/			
U.S. No. 2 yellow soybeans	252	247	237
U.S. 44 % soybean meal	NQ	NQ	NQ
Brazil 48 % soy pellets	203	201	208
U.S. Farm Prices 3/ 4/			
Wheat	91	99	137
Barley	73	75	79
Corn	97	100	89
Sorghum	89	91	87
Broiler 5/	1,223	1,360	1,289
Soybeans 6/	225	217	227
EC Import Levies			
Common wheat	119	117	120
Durum wheat	141	132	176
Barley	105	105	176
Corn	110	111	125
Sorghum	118	114	163
Broilers	262	270	NA
EC Export Restitution (subsidies)8/			
Common wheat	73	61	24
Barley	90	71	115
Broilers	276	285	43

NQ = No quote. NA = Not available. Note: Changes in dollar value of EC import levies, intervention prices, and export restitutions may be the result of changes in $/ECU exchange rates.

*1/ Mid-week quote. 2/ Asking price in dollars for imported grain and soybeans and soybean products, c.i.f. Rotterdam for nearby delivery. 3/ Five-day moving average. 4/ Target price for current marketing year in $/metric ton: wheat, $151; barley, $112; corn, $112; sorghum, $106; soybean loan rate, $166. 5/ Composite 12-city weighted average price for trucklot sales to be delivered to first receiver. 6/ Central Illinois processors bid to arrive. 7/ Buy-in equals 94% of intervention price plus full value of monthly increments. 8/ Figures represent restitutions awarded nearest to the listed dates, * denotes no award given since the previous month.*

Note: The EC intervention prices, which are usually included in this table, will resume in November when the EC begins buying-in.

UNITED STATES DEPARTMENT OF AGRICULTURE
WASHINGTON, D.C. 20250

OFFICIAL BUSINESS
PENALTY FOR PRIVATE USE, $300

If your address should be changed_____PRINT
OR TYPE the new address, including ZIP CODE and
return the whole sheet and/or envelope to:

FOREIGN AGRICULTURAL SERVICE, Room 4644 So.
U.S. Department of Agriculture
Washington, D.C. 20250

Important Notice to Readers --

Agricultural Trade Highlights is available on a subscription basis only. The subscri
fee is $15 in the United States or $23 for foreign addressees. To subscribe, send
check, payable to the Foreign Agricultural Service, to: Information Division, FAS, U
Room 4644-South Building, Washington, D.C. 20250-1000. Only checks drawn or
banks, or international money orders will be accepted. NO REFUNDS CAI
MADE.

This publication is a product of the Trade and Economic Information Division, F
Agricultural Service, U.S. Department of Agriculture, Room 6506-South Bui
Washington, D.C. 20250-1000. Questions on the subject matter of this report shou
directed to Mike Dwyer at (202) 382-1294.

CPSIA information can be obtained
at www.ICGtesting.com
Printed in the USA
LVHW050033271118
598300LV00027B/993/P